WIX WEBSITE FOR BEGINNERS

A Comprehensive Guide to Building Your First Website with Wix

Ryan Howarth

CONTENTS

INTRODUCTION

Importance of Having a Professional Website

In today's digital age, having a professional website is essential for businesses, entrepreneurs, and professionals across various industries. A website serves as a virtual storefront, allowing individuals and organizations to showcase their products, services, and expertise to a global audience. Here are several key reasons why having a professional website is of utmost importance.

1. Online Presence and Credibility: A professional website establishes your online presence, enabling potential customers and clients to find you easily. In the digital era, consumers often turn to the internet to research products, services, or professionals before making a purchase or decision. Having a well-designed website with valuable content enhances your credibility and instills trust in your target audience.

2. Branding and Differentiation: A professional website allows you to shape and communicate your brand identity effectively. It serves as a platform to showcase your unique selling proposition, values, and visual elements that differentiate you from competitors. With a well-designed website, you can create a memorable and consistent brand experience that resonates with your target market.

3. Increased Reach and Customer Acquisition: A website expands your reach beyond geographical boundaries. It enables potential customers from all over the world to discover your business or services, significantly increasing your customer acquisition potential. With proper search engine optimization (SEO) techniques, your website can rank higher in search engine results, driving organic traffic and attracting relevant visitors.

4. 24/7 Availability and Accessibility: Unlike traditional brick-and-mortar establishments with limited operating hours, a website is available round the clock. It allows visitors to access information, make inquiries, or purchase products or services at their convenience. This accessibility enhances customer satisfaction and leads to increased conversions and sales.

5. Showcase Products and Services: A professional website provides an ideal platform to showcase your offerings. You can feature high-quality images, detailed descriptions, and even videos to demonstrate the value and benefits of your products or services. This visual representation helps potential customers make informed decisions and increases their likelihood of engaging with your business.

6. Enhanced Customer Support: Your website can serve as a hub for customer support and engagement. You can provide FAQs, knowledge bases, or even live chat features to address customer inquiries promptly. By offering excellent customer support through your website, you build stronger relationships with your audience and foster customer loyalty.

7. Data Analytics and Insights: A professional website integrated with analytics tools provides valuable insights into your audience's behavior and preferences. You can track visitor demographics, browsing patterns, and engagement metrics to make data-driven decisions. These insights help you optimize your website, content, and marketing strategies for better results.

8. Competitive Advantage: In today's competitive landscape, having a professional website sets you apart from businesses that rely solely on traditional marketing methods. A well-designed website with a seamless user experience showcases your commitment to innovation and staying relevant in a digital-first world. It gives you a competitive edge and positions you as a leader in your industry.

9. Cost-Effectiveness: Compared to traditional advertising and marketing channels, having a professional website offers a cost-effective solution. While there might be initial investments in web design and development, hosting, and maintenance, the long-term benefits outweigh the costs. A website serves as a long-lasting marketing asset, requiring minimal ongoing expenses.

In conclusion, having a professional website is no longer optional but a necessity in today's digital landscape. It enables businesses and professionals to establish their online presence, build credibility, reach a broader audience, and showcase their offerings effectively. With the numerous advantages it offers, investing in a professional website is a strategic decision that can lead to substantial growth and success.

Overview of Wix Platform

Wix is a popular website builder and hosting platform that empowers individuals and businesses to create professional websites without the need for coding or technical expertise. It provides a user-friendly interface and a wide range of customizable templates and features, making it accessible to beginners and experienced users alike. Here is an overview of the key components and functionalities of the Wix platform.

1. Website Creation: Wix offers a drag-and-drop website editor that simplifies the process of building a website. Users can choose from a vast collection of professionally designed templates categorized by industry or purpose. The intuitive editor allows customization of layout, design elements, colors, fonts, and more, ensuring flexibility and creative freedom.

2. Mobile Optimization: With the increasing number of users accessing the internet through mobile devices, Wix provides mobile optimization features to ensure a seamless user experience across different screen sizes. Users can preview and adjust their website's appearance on mobile devices to deliver an optimized experience to their mobile visitors.

3. App Market: Wix offers an extensive App Market that provides additional functionality and integrations for websites. Users can browse and install various apps, such as contact forms, social media feeds, e-commerce solutions, booking systems, and more, to enhance their website's capabilities and meet specific business requirements.

4. E-commerce Solutions: Wix provides robust e-commerce features, allowing users to create and manage online stores with ease. Users can add product listings, set up payment gateways, manage inventory, configure shipping options, and track orders. The platform supports various e-commerce functionalities, making it suitable for businesses of all sizes.

5. SEO Optimization: Wix incorporates SEO tools and features to help users improve their website's visibility in search engine results. Users can optimize page titles, meta descriptions, URLs, and alt tags for images, enhancing their chances of ranking higher in search engine rankings. The platform also provides built-in SEO guides and analytics to track website performance.

6. Blogging Capabilities: Wix includes built-in blogging functionality, allowing users to create and manage blog posts within their websites. Users can customize blog layouts, schedule posts, enable comments, and promote their content through social sharing buttons. This feature is beneficial for individuals, businesses, or professionals aiming to share valuable content and establish thought leadership.

7. Analytics and Insights: Wix provides analytics tools that offer valuable insights into website performance and visitor behavior. Users can track metrics such as page views, visitor demographics, traffic sources, and more. These analytics enable data-driven decision-making, allowing users to optimize their websites and marketing strategies for better results.

8. Hosting and Security: Wix provides secure and reliable hosting for websites built on its platform. Users don't need to worry about server maintenance, security updates, or backups, as Wix takes care of these technical aspects.

The platform also offers SSL encryption for secure data transmission and integrates with third-party security solutions for added protection.

In summary, Wix is a comprehensive website building and hosting platform that empowers users to create professional and feature-rich websites without the need for coding skills. With its intuitive interface, extensive customization options, and diverse functionalities, Wix caters to a wide range of users, from individuals and small businesses to large enterprises. Whether you're looking to create a simple portfolio website, an online store, or a blog, Wix provides the tools and resources to bring your vision to life.

Purpose of the Ebook

1. Knowledge Sharing and Education: eBooks serve as a powerful tool for knowledge sharing and education. They allow authors to delve into a specific topic, providing in-depth information, insights, and analysis. eBooks can be used to educate readers on various subjects, including self-help, business strategies, industry trends, academic topics, and more. The purpose of an educational eBook is to empower readers with valuable knowledge and equip them with the skills needed to succeed in their respective fields.

2. **Lead Generation and Marketing:** eBooks are often used as a lead generation and marketing tool by businesses and professionals. By offering a free or discounted eBook in exchange for a reader's contact information, such as their email address, authors can build their subscriber list and nurture leads. The eBook acts as an incentive, attracting potential customers and positioning the author as an authority in their industry. It serves as a stepping stone for further engagement and potential business opportunities.

3. **Thought Leadership and Branding:** Publishing an eBook allows individuals and businesses to establish themselves as thought leaders in their respective domains. By sharing valuable insights, original research, or innovative ideas, authors can position themselves as experts and gain credibility within their industry. The purpose of a thought leadership eBook is to elevate the author's reputation, enhance their personal or brand image, and attract attention from peers, clients, or customers.

4. **Content Monetization:** eBooks can serve as a source of

revenue for authors. Whether self-published or through established publishing platforms, authors can sell their eBooks to generate income. This is particularly beneficial for subject matter experts, writers, and entrepreneurs who have valuable content to share and a target audience willing to invest in acquiring that knowledge. The purpose of a monetized eBook is to provide valuable content while also creating a source of income for the author.

5. Storytelling and Entertainment: eBooks can be used as a medium for storytelling and entertainment purposes. Fiction authors utilize eBooks to engage readers in captivating narratives, imaginative worlds, and compelling characters. These eBooks aim to entertain, engage emotions, and provide an immersive reading experience. Non-fiction authors can also use storytelling techniques to present information in a more engaging and relatable manner, making complex topics more accessible to readers.

6. Building Authority and Influence: An eBook can help authors build authority and influence within their industry or niche. By sharing their expertise, experiences, and unique perspectives, authors can attract a dedicated following and become recognized as a trusted source of information. The purpose of an authority-building eBook is to establish the author's credibility, expand their professional network, and open doors to speaking engagements, consulting opportunities, or collaborations.

7. **Promoting Products or Services:** eBooks can be used as a promotional tool to showcase and highlight products or services offered by a business. Authors can include case studies, success stories, or practical tips related to their offerings within the eBook. The purpose is to demonstrate the value and benefits of their products or services to potential customers and encourage them to take action, such as making a purchase or signing up for a consultation.

8. **Creating Awareness and Advocacy:** eBooks can be instrumental in creating awareness and advocacy for specific causes, social issues, or initiatives. Authors can use eBooks to educate readers, raise awareness about important topics, and inspire action. The purpose is to mobilize readers, drive positive change, and foster a sense of community around a shared cause.

CHAPTER ONE

Understanding Wix

What is Wix?

Wix is a popular cloud-based website development platform that allows users to create stunning websites without any coding knowledge. It was founded in 2006 by Avishai Abrahami, Nadav Abrahami, and Giora Kaplan. With its intuitive drag-and-drop editor, Wix has gained immense popularity and currently hosts millions of websites across various industries.

Wix offers a user-friendly interface that enables individuals, small businesses, and even large enterprises to build their online presence easily. Whether you want to create a personal blog, an e-commerce store, or a professional portfolio, Wix provides all the necessary tools and features to bring your vision to life.

Features and Benefits of Wix

Wix comes equipped with a wide range of features and benefits that make it a preferred choice for website creation. Let's explore some of its key features:

1. **Drag-and-Drop Editor:** Wix's drag-and-drop editor allows users to customize their website design effortlessly. You can simply select elements from the sidebar and drop them onto your page, rearrange them, resize them, and personalize their appearance according to your preferences.

2. **Templates and Design Flexibility:** Wix offers a vast collection of professionally designed templates for various industries and niches. These templates serve as a starting point for your website and can be fully customized to match your branding. Whether you want a sleek and modern look or a vibrant and colorful design, Wix provides the flexibility to achieve your desired aesthetic.

3. **Mobile Optimization:** With the increasing use of mobile devices, it is crucial for websites to be mobile-friendly. Wix automatically optimizes your website for mobile viewing, ensuring a seamless experience for visitors on smartphones and tablets.

4. **App Market:** Wix has an extensive App Market that allows you to enhance your

website's functionality with various add-ons and integrations. From e-commerce tools to marketing plugins, you can easily expand your website's capabilities to suit your specific needs.

5. **SEO Optimization:** Wix provides built-in SEO features to help improve your website's visibility on search engines. You can customize meta tags, titles, and descriptions for each page, making it easier for search engines to crawl and index your content.

6. **Wix ADI (Artificial Design Intelligence):** For users who prefer a more automated approach, Wix ADI offers an intelligent solution. By answering a few questions about your website's purpose and design preferences, Wix ADI generates a personalized website design and layout, saving you time and effort.

7. **Hosting and Security:** Wix handles website hosting, ensuring reliable and secure performance. They also provide SSL certificates to encrypt data transmitted between your website and visitors, enhancing security and trust.

Wix Pricing Plans

Wix offers various pricing plans tailored to different needs and budgets. Here are the key pricing tiers:

1. **Free Plan:** Wix offers a free plan that allows you to create a basic website with Wix branding. While this plan is suitable for personal use and exploration, it comes with limitations such as

displaying Wix ads and not having a custom domain.

2. **Combo Plan:** The Combo plan is ideal for personal use or small businesses. It includes features like a custom domain, removal of Wix ads, additional storage and bandwidth, and access to customer support. This plan is suitable for those who want a more professional online presence without breaking the bank.

3. **Unlimited Plan:** The Unlimited plan is designed for entrepreneurs and freelancers who require more resources. It offers unlimited bandwidth, additional storage, a professional logo, and a Site Booster app to enhance website visibility.

4. **Pro Plan:** The Pro plan is geared towards small businesses and provides additional features such as VIP customer support, the ability to accept online payments, and access to advanced design capabilities.

5. **VIP Plan:** The VIP plan offers priority support, VIP priority response, and a professional site review to ensure your website meets high-quality standards. It is suitable for businesses that require a premium level of support and personalized attention.

It's important to note that Wix frequently offers promotional discounts and deals, so it's worth checking their website for the most up-to-date pricing information.

CHAPTER TWO

Getting Started with Wix

Setting Up Your Wix Account

Setting up a Wix account is a straightforward process that allows you to create and manage your own website. Wix is a user-friendly platform that offers a wide range of templates and customization options. To get started, follow these steps:

1. **Create an Account:** Visit the Wix website and click on the "Sign Up" button. You can sign up using your email address or through social media accounts like Facebook or Google.

2. **Choose a Plan:** Wix offers different plans, including a free plan with limited features and paid plans with more advanced options. Select a plan that suits your needs and budget. You can always upgrade to a paid plan later if required.

3. **Select a Domain Name:** A domain name is the

address of your website. Wix allows you to choose a domain name with the extension ".wixsite.com" for free. Alternatively, you can purchase a custom domain name for a more professional look.

4. **Set Up Your Website:** After choosing your domain name, you'll be directed to the Wix Editor, where you can start building your website. Wix provides a drag-and-drop interface, making it easy to add and customize elements on your site.

Choosing a Template

When setting up your Wix account, one of the crucial decisions you'll make is selecting a template. Templates serve as a foundation for your website design and determine its overall look and feel. Here's how you can choose the right template:

1. **Browse the Template Gallery:** Wix offers an extensive collection of templates across various industries and categories. Take the time to explore different options and find a template that aligns with your website's purpose and target audience.

2. **Consider Functionality:** Templates on Wix are designed with specific functionalities in mind, such as e-commerce, blogging, photography, or portfolios. Consider the features you require for your website and select a template that supports those functionalities.

3. **Evaluate Design Elements:** Pay attention to the layout, color scheme, and typography of each

template. Look for a design that represents your brand and appeals to your target audience. Customization options are available later, but starting with a template that already resonates with your vision saves time.

4. **Mobile Responsiveness:** In today's mobile-driven world, it's crucial to choose a template that is mobile-responsive. Wix templates are optimized for mobile devices, ensuring your website looks great on smartphones and tablets.

Customizing Your Website

Wix provides extensive customization options, allowing you to personalize your website and make it truly your own. Here are some key steps to customize your Wix website:

1. **Edit Text and Images:** Easily modify the text and images on your website by clicking on them in the Wix Editor. You can change fonts, colors, sizes, and even add effects. Replace the default content with your own text and high-quality images.

2. **Add New Elements:** Wix offers a wide range of elements you can add to your website, such as galleries, videos, contact forms, and social media icons. Drag and drop these elements onto your pages and customize them according to your

needs.

3. **Navigation Menu:** Customize your website's navigation menu to make it easy for visitors to navigate through your site. Add or remove menu items, create drop-down menus, and arrange the order of pages.

4. **Apps and Integrations:** Enhance your website's functionality by adding apps and integrations. Wix has an App Market where you can explore and install various third-party apps to extend the capabilities of your website.

Logo and Branding

Your website's logo and branding play a vital role in establishing your online identity and creating a memorable impression. Here's how you can create a logo and maintain consistent branding on Wix:

1. **Design a Logo:** Wix offers a user-friendly logo maker tool called Wix Logo Maker. It allows you to create a professional-looking logo tailored to your brand. Alternatively, you can upload your own logo if you already have one.

2. **Brand Colors:** Choose a color palette that aligns with your brand identity and use it consistently across your website. Wix makes it easy to customize colors, ensuring a cohesive and visually appealing design.

3. **Typography:** Select appropriate fonts that reflect your brand's personality and ensure readability.

Wix provides a wide range of fonts to choose from, allowing you to find the perfect match for your website.

4. **Consistency:** Maintain consistency in your branding elements throughout your website. Use your logo, colors, and fonts consistently across all pages and sections to create a unified and professional look.

Color Scheme and Typography

The color scheme and typography choices have a significant impact on the overall visual appeal and user experience of your website. Consider the following points when selecting color schemes and typography on Wix:

1. **Color Psychology:** Different colors evoke specific emotions and associations. Consider the psychological effects of colors and choose a color scheme that aligns with the mood and message you want to convey. For example, blue conveys trust and reliability, while yellow represents energy and optimism.

2. **Contrast and Readability:** Ensure there is enough contrast between the background and text colors for optimal readability. Avoid using light text on a light background or dark text on a dark background. Test different color combinations to find the right balance.

3. **Typography Hierarchy:** Establish a typography hierarchy by assigning different font styles and

sizes to different types of content. Use larger and bolder fonts for headings and titles, and more readable fonts for body text. Consistency in typography throughout the website maintains a professional look.

4. **Legibility and Accessibility:** Choose fonts that are legible and easy to read across different devices and screen sizes. Consider accessibility guidelines and ensure your chosen fonts meet the necessary standards.

Layout and Structure

The layout and structure of your website are essential for a seamless user experience and effective communication of your content. Consider the following aspects when working on the layout and structure on Wix:

1. **Grid-Based Layout:** Use a grid-based layout to create a well-organized and visually pleasing design. Align elements to the grid, maintaining consistency and a sense of order.

2. **Whitespace:** Incorporate whitespace strategically to provide breathing room for your content. Whitespace helps in emphasizing key elements and enhances readability.

3. **Page Hierarchy:** Establish a clear hierarchy of pages and sections. Ensure important information is easily accessible and that visitors can navigate through your website intuitively.

4. **Responsive Design:** Wix templates are optimized

for responsiveness, meaning your website will adapt to different screen sizes and devices. However, it's essential to review and test your website's responsiveness to ensure a consistent experience across platforms.

CHAPTER THREE

Building Your Website

Adding and Editing Pages

When it comes to building a website, adding and editing pages is an essential task. It allows you to create a well-structured website with relevant content. Whether you're a business owner, blogger, or an aspiring web developer, understanding how to add and edit pages is crucial. In this section, we will explore the process of adding and editing pages, focusing on the following topics: Home Page, About Us Page, Products/Services Page, and Contact Us Page.

Home Page

The home page is the first impression visitors get of your website, so it's important to make it captivating and engaging. When adding and editing the home page, consider the following points:

1. Clear and Concise Introduction: Start by introducing your website's purpose and what sets it apart from others. Keep the content concise and captivating to grab the visitors' attention.

2. Call to Action: Include a clear call to action to guide visitors to take the desired action, such as signing up for a newsletter or exploring your products/services.

3. Engaging Visuals: Incorporate high-quality images or videos that resonate with your brand and capture the visitors' interest. Visuals can help convey your message effectively.

4. Navigation Menu: Ensure that your home page includes a well-structured navigation menu, making it easy for visitors to explore other pages of your website.

About Us Page

The About Us page provides an opportunity to tell your website visitors more about your brand, values, and mission. Here are some key points to consider when adding and editing the About Us page:

1. **Brand Story:** Share the story behind your brand, including its inception, milestones, and any unique experiences that shaped your business. Use a storytelling approach to engage your audience.

2. **Team Introduction:** Introduce key team members, highlighting their expertise and roles within the organization. Including personal anecdotes or achievements can help build trust and humanize your brand.

3. **Values and Mission:** Clearly communicate your brand's values and mission. Explain how these principles guide your business decisions and differentiate you from competitors.

4. **Testimonials or Success Stories:** Feature testimonials or success stories from satisfied customers or clients. This can help build credibility and showcase the positive impact your products or services have had on others.

Products/Services Page

The Products/Services page is where you showcase what you have to offer. It should provide comprehensive information about your offerings and convince visitors to become customers. Consider the following when adding and editing the Products/Services page:

1. **Clear Product/Service Descriptions:** Clearly describe each product or service you offer, including its features, benefits, and unique selling points. Use persuasive language to highlight how your offerings can solve customers' problems or fulfill their needs.

2. **Pricing and Packages:** If applicable, provide pricing information and details about different packages or tiers available. Make the pricing structure easy to understand and consider offering options that cater to different budgets.

3. **Visuals and Media:** Include high-quality images, videos, or interactive media that showcase your products or services in action. Visual representations can significantly impact a visitor's decision-making process.

4. **Testimonials or Case Studies:** Incorporate testimonials or case studies that demonstrate the positive outcomes

your products or services have achieved for previous customers. This can instill trust and confidence in potential buyers.

Contact Us Page

The Contact Us page is a crucial component of your website as it allows visitors to get in touch with you. When adding and editing the Contact Us page, focus on the following aspects:

1. Contact Information: Provide clear and visible contact information, including your business's address, phone number, email address, and social media profiles. Make it easy for visitors to reach out to you through their preferred communication channel.

2. Contact Form: Consider adding a contact form to simplify the process for visitors to send inquiries or messages. Keep the form fields concise and relevant to avoid overwhelming users.

3. Map and Directions: If you have a physical location, embed a map or provide directions to help visitors find your business easily. This is especially important for local businesses or establishments.

4. Response Time: Clearly communicate the expected response time for inquiries. Promptly responding to messages helps build trust and demonstrates your commitment to customer satisfaction.

Navigation and Menus

Effective navigation and menus are vital for providing a seamless browsing experience on your website. Here are some considerations for adding and managing navigation and menus:

1. Clear and Intuitive Structure: Design a logical navigation structure that helps visitors find the information they need effortlessly. Categorize your pages and group related content under suitable headings.

2. User-Friendly Menu Design: Use clear labels for menu items and ensure they are easily visible. Consider using drop-down menus or mega menus to accommodate a larger number of pages or subcategories.

3. Consistency: Maintain consistent navigation across all pages to prevent confusion. Visitors should easily recognize and access the main menu, regardless of their location on the website.

4. Mobile Responsiveness: Optimize your navigation and menus for mobile devices. Consider implementing a responsive design that adapts to different screen sizes, ensuring a user-friendly experience on smartphones and tablets.

Adding and Formatting Text

Text content plays a crucial role in conveying information and engaging visitors. When adding and formatting text on your website, keep the following points in mind:

1. Clear and Readable Typography: Choose fonts that are legible and easy to read. Use appropriate font sizes, line spacing, and contrast to enhance readability. Consider using headings, subheadings, and bullet points to organize the text.

2. Consistent Formatting: Maintain consistency in formatting throughout the website. Use the same font styles, sizes, and colors across pages to create a cohesive look and feel.

3. Emphasis and Hierarchy: Use formatting techniques such as bold, italics, or underlining to emphasize important information or key points. Establish a clear hierarchy to guide visitors' attention and make the content scannable.

4. SEO Optimization: Incorporate relevant keywords within the text to improve search engine optimization. However, prioritize natural and meaningful content over keyword stuffing.

Inserting Images and Videos

Images and videos are powerful visual elements that can enhance your website's overall appeal and engagement. Consider the following when inserting and managing media content:

1. High-Quality Visuals: Use high-resolution images and videos that are relevant to your content. Ensure the media files are optimized for web usage to avoid slow loading times.

2. Captions and Alt Text: Provide descriptive captions for images and use alt text to describe the content of the media files. This improves accessibility for visually impaired users and assists search engines in understanding the context.

3. Proper Placement: Insert images and videos

strategically to support the surrounding text or convey a specific message. Consider alignment, size, and positioning for optimal visual impact.

4. Video Hosting and Embedding: If you're using videos, choose a reliable video hosting platform or service. Embed the videos using the appropriate embed codes or plugins for seamless playback.

Integrating Widgets and Apps

Widgets and apps can add additional functionality and interactivity to your website. Here's what to consider when integrating widgets and apps:

1. **Purpose and Relevance:** Select widgets and apps that serve a specific purpose and align with your website's
2. **Compatibility and Performance:** Ensure that the widgets and apps you integrate are compatible with your website's platform or content management system. Test their performance to ensure they don't slow down your website's loading speed.
3. **User Experience:** Consider how the widgets and apps will enhance the overall user experience. Avoid cluttering the website with too many widgets or apps, as it can distract or overwhelm visitors.

4. **Customization:** Look for widgets and apps that offer customization options, allowing you to match their appearance with your website's design and branding.

5. **Security and Updates:** Prioritize widgets and apps that have regular updates and security measures in place. It's crucial to protect your website and its visitors from potential vulnerabilities.

Integrating widgets and apps can greatly enhance the functionality and user experience of your website. Choose wisely and ensure they align with your website's goals and audience.

Adding and editing pages, along with managing navigation, formatting text, inserting media, and integrating widgets and apps, are essential skills for creating a well-rounded and dynamic website. Remember to prioritize clarity, user experience, and consistency throughout your website. Regularly review and update your content to keep it fresh and relevant.

By mastering these skills, you'll be well-equipped to create a professional and engaging website that effectively communicates your message and meets the needs of your target audience.

Remember to experiment, learn from user feedback, and

stay updated with the latest trends and best practices in web design and content management. Building a successful website is an ongoing process that requires continuous improvement and adaptation.

CHAPTER FOUR

Enhancing Your Website

Optimizing for Search Engines (SEO)

Search Engine Optimization (SEO) is a crucial aspect of any website's success. It involves optimizing a website's content and structure to improve its visibility and ranking in search engine results. Effective SEO practices can lead to increased organic traffic, better user engagement, and higher conversions. Here are some key strategies for optimizing your website for search engines:

1. Keyword Research and Optimization

Keywords are the foundation of SEO. Conduct thorough research to identify relevant keywords and phrases that your target audience is likely to use when searching for information related to your website's content. Include these keywords strategically in your website's meta tags, titles, headings, URLs, and throughout the content. However, avoid keyword stuffing, as it can lead to penalties from search engines.

2. High-Quality Content

Creating high-quality, valuable content is essential for both users and search engines. Develop informative and engaging content that addresses the needs and interests of your target audience. Use proper formatting, such as headings, subheadings, and bullet points, to enhance readability. Incorporate relevant keywords naturally within the content, while ensuring it flows smoothly and provides value to the reader.

3. Website Structure and Navigation

A well-structured website enhances user experience and improves search engine crawling and indexing. Organize your website's content into logical sections and use descriptive URLs, making it easier for search engines to understand and index your pages. Implement a clear navigation system that allows users to find information quickly and easily. Use internal linking to establish connections between related pages and improve overall website visibility.

4. Mobile Optimization

In today's mobile-driven world, optimizing your website for mobile devices is crucial. Mobile optimization ensures that your website is responsive and displays correctly across various screen sizes and devices. Search engines prioritize mobile-friendly websites, so optimizing for mobile can significantly improve your search engine rankings. Make sure your website loads quickly, images are optimized for mobile, and the content is easily readable on smaller screens.

5. Page Speed Optimization

Page speed is a critical factor in SEO. Slow-loading websites can negatively impact user experience and lead to higher bounce rates. Optimize your website's performance by minimizing file sizes, compressing images, and leveraging browser caching. Regularly monitor and optimize your website's loading speed to provide a seamless browsing experience and improve search engine rankings.

6. Link Building

Link building is an essential off-page SEO technique. It involves acquiring high-quality backlinks from other reputable websites. Backlinks act as votes of confidence for search engines, indicating the authority and relevance of your website. Develop a link-building strategy that focuses on obtaining links from authoritative sources within your industry. This can be achieved through guest blogging, content promotion, influencer collaborations, and networking with other website owners.

7. Monitoring and Analytics

Continuously monitor and analyze your website's performance using tools like Google Analytics. Track important metrics such as organic traffic, bounce rate, average session duration, and conversion rates. Analyzing this data can provide valuable insights into user behavior and help identify areas for improvement. Regularly review and adjust your SEO strategy based on the data to ensure optimal results.

Mobile Optimization

In the era of smartphones and tablets, optimizing your website for mobile devices is crucial to deliver a seamless user experience. Here are some key considerations for mobile optimization:

1. Responsive Design: Implement a responsive design that automatically adjusts the layout and content to fit different screen sizes. This ensures that your website looks and functions well across various devices.

2. Mobile-Friendly Navigation: Simplify your website's navigation for mobile users. Use clear and intuitive menus, icons, and buttons that are easy to tap and navigate with a touchscreen.

3. Clear Call-to-Action: Make your call-to-action buttons prominent and easily accessible on mobile devices. Ensure they are large enough to tap with a finger without accidentally pressing neighboring elements.

4. Optimized Images: Optimize images for mobile by compressing file sizes without compromising quality. Large image files can significantly slow down page loading speed on mobile devices.

5. Accelerated Mobile Pages (AMP): Consider implementing AMP, a Google-backed technology that improves mobile page loading speed. AMP pages are stripped-down versions of your website's content, designed to load quickly on mobile devices.

6. Mobile-Specific SEO: Pay attention to mobile-

specific SEO techniques, such as optimizing for voice search and local search. Voice search is becoming increasingly popular, and optimizing your website for voice queries can improve your visibility in mobile search results.

7. User Testing: Test your website on various mobile devices and screen sizes to ensure it functions correctly and provides a positive user experience. Identify any issues or usability problems and address them promptly.

Adding E-commerce Functionality

Integrating e-commerce functionality into your website allows you to sell products or services online, expanding your business opportunities. Here are some steps to consider when adding e-commerce functionality:

1. Choose an E-commerce Platform: Select an e-commerce platform that suits your business needs. Popular options include Shopify, WooCommerce, Magento, and BigCommerce. Consider factors such as ease of use, customization options, scalability, and payment gateway integrations.

2. Product Management: Organize your products into categories and subcategories. Include detailed product descriptions, high-quality images, and relevant specifications. Implement a search functionality and filtering options to enhance the user's browsing experience.

3. **Secure Payment Gateway Integration:** Integrate a secure payment gateway that supports various payment methods. Ensure that customers' financial information is protected and comply with industry standards and regulations, such as PCI-DSS.

4. **Shopping Cart and Checkout:** Implement a user-friendly shopping cart system that allows customers to add products, review their order, and proceed to checkout seamlessly. Simplify the checkout process by minimizing the number of steps required to complete a purchase.

5. **Order Management:** Set up an order management system to track and process customer orders efficiently. Provide order confirmation emails, shipping notifications, and options for customer feedback or support.

6. **Security Measures:** Implement SSL encryption to secure customer data during the checkout process. Display trust badges and security seals to instill confidence in your

customers.

7. Marketing and Promotion: Develop a marketing strategy to promote your e-commerce store. Utilize digital marketing techniques such as search engine optimization (SEO), social media marketing, email marketing, and paid advertising to drive traffic and increase conversions.

Implementing Social Media Integration

Social media integration allows you to leverage the power of social platforms to enhance your website's visibility and engage with your audience. Here are some ways to implement social media integration effectively:

1. Social Sharing Buttons: Add social sharing buttons to your website's content, making it easy for users to share your articles, products, or any other valuable content with their social media networks. This can help increase your content's reach and generate more traffic.

2. Social Login: Offer the option for users to log in or sign up using their social media accounts. This simplifies the registration process, eliminates the need to create new accounts, and encourages user participation.

3. Social Media Feeds: Embed social media feeds on your

website to showcase your social media presence and recent updates. This can help establish credibility and encourage users to follow or engage with your social media accounts.

4. **Social Media Widgets:** Incorporate social media widgets that display your follower count, likes, shares, or testimonials directly on your website. This social proof can build trust and credibility among visitors.

5. **Social Media Commenting:** Enable social media commenting on your blog posts or other content. This allows users to comment using their social media accounts, increasing engagement and encouraging discussions.

6. **Social Media Integration in E-commerce:** Integrate social media into your e-commerce store by allowing customers to share their purchases on social platforms, providing social login options during the checkout process, and showcasing user-generated content related to your products.

7. **Social Media Advertising:** Utilize social media advertising platforms to reach a wider audience. Platforms like Facebook Ads, Instagram Ads, and Twitter Ads allow you to target specific demographics, interests, and

behaviors to increase brand awareness and drive traffic to your website.

By effectively implementing social media integration, you can extend your online presence, engage with your audience, and leverage the power of social media to enhance your website's visibility and reach.

Adding Forms and Collecting Data

Forms are a valuable tool for collecting data, generating leads, and engaging with your website visitors. Here's how you can add forms and effectively collect data:

1. Identify Your Goals: Determine the purpose of your forms. Are you collecting leads, conducting surveys, or allowing users to contact you? Clarifying your goals helps you create targeted and relevant forms.

2. Select a Form Builder: Choose a user-friendly form builder tool that suits your requirements. Popular options include Gravity Forms, Wufoo, Google Forms, and Typeform. These tools provide drag-and-drop interfaces and offer a variety of form field options.

3. Design and Placement: Design visually appealing forms that align with your website's aesthetics. Place the forms strategically on relevant pages to maximize visibility and user engagement. Consider using pop-up or slide-in forms to grab attention.

4. Form Fields and Validation: Determine the necessary form fields for capturing the desired data. Keep the form concise and easy to fill out. Implement validation rules to ensure accurate and valid data entry.

5. Calls-to-Action (CTAs): Use compelling CTAs to encourage users to fill out your forms. Clearly communicate the benefits or incentives users will receive by providing their information.

6. Privacy and Data Protection: Clearly communicate your privacy policy and assure users that their data will be protected. Implement necessary security measures, such as SSL encryption, to secure sensitive information.

7. Data Management and Automation: Integrate your form with a data management system or customer relationship management (CRM) software. This allows you to organize and automate data collection, follow-up processes, and lead nurturing.

By adding forms to your website and effectively collecting

data, you can gain valuable insights about your audience, generate leads, and enhance your overall marketing efforts.

Incorporating Blogs and Newsletters

Blogs and newsletters are powerful tools for content marketing, establishing thought leadership, and engaging with your audience. Here's how you can incorporate blogs and newsletters effectively:

1. Content Strategy: Develop a content strategy that aligns with your target audience's interests and needs. Determine the topics, tone, and frequency of your blog posts and newsletters. Consistency is key to maintaining reader engagement.

2. Blog Design and Layout: Design a visually appealing and user-friendly blog layout. Ensure it is easy to navigate, search, and share content. Incorporate relevant visuals, such as images, infographics, or videos, to enhance the reader's experience.

3. SEO Optimization: Optimize your blog posts for search engines by conducting keyword research and incorporating relevant keywords naturally into your content. Use proper headings, meta tags, and alt tags for images to improve search engine visibility.

4. Engaging Content: Create high-quality, informative, and engaging blog posts that provide value to your readers. Use storytelling, examples, and actionable tips to make your content memorable and shareable.

5. Call-to-Action (CTA): Include CTAs within your blog posts to encourage reader engagement and conversion. These CTAs can be inviting readers to subscribe to your newsletter, download a resource, or explore your products or services.

6. Newsletter Design and Personalization: Design visually appealing and mobile-friendly newsletters. Personalize the content and address subscribers by their names. Use an engaging subject line to increase open rates.

7. Email Marketing Automation: Utilize email marketing automation tools to schedule and send newsletters at regular intervals. Segment your subscriber list based on their interests or demographics for targeted communication.

By incorporating blogs and newsletters into your website, you can establish your brand as a valuable source of information, nurture relationships with your audience, and drive traffic to your website.

Remember, optimizing for search engines, mobile devices, integrating e-commerce functionality, incorporating social media, adding forms, and leveraging blogs and newsletters are essential strategies to enhance your website's visibility, user experience, and overall online success. Implementing these strategies can help you reach a wider audience, increase conversions, and achieve your business goals.

CHAPTER FIVE

Advanced Features and Tips

Wix Code and Advanced Customization

Wix is a popular website builder that offers a range of features and tools for creating and customizing websites. One of the key features of Wix is its advanced customization options, which allow users to take their websites to the next level. With Wix Code, users can access the platform's built-in development environment and create custom functionalities and dynamic pages. This opens up a world of possibilities for those looking to build more interactive and dynamic websites.

Wix Code Features

Wix Code provides several features that enable advanced customization. These include:

1. **Database Integration**: Wix Code allows users to create and manage their own databases directly within the platform. This feature is especially useful for websites that require dynamic content, such as e-commerce sites or event management platforms. Users can easily store and retrieve data, create custom forms, and connect their databases to different elements on their website.

2. **API Access**: With Wix Code, users have the ability to connect external APIs to their websites. This enables the integration of third-party services, such as payment gateways, social media platforms, or email marketing tools. By leveraging APIs, users can extend the functionality of their websites and create seamless user experiences.

3. **Custom Interactions**: Wix Code allows users to create custom interactions using JavaScript. This means that users can add unique animations, effects, and behaviors to their website elements. By writing custom code, users can control how different elements on their site respond to user interactions, creating a more engaging and interactive experience.

4. **Dynamic Pages**: Wix Code enables the creation of dynamic pages, where content is generated on the fly based on user input or database queries. This is particularly useful for websites that have large amounts of content or frequently updated information. Users can design templates and set up rules that determine how dynamic content is displayed, providing a personalized experience for their visitors.

Benefits of Advanced Customization with Wix Code

The advanced customization options provided by Wix Code offer several benefits to website owners:

1. **Flexibility**: With Wix Code, users have the flexibility to create custom functionalities and tailor their websites to meet specific requirements. Whether it's integrating a custom payment system, building a complex form, or creating interactive elements, Wix Code provides the tools to bring ideas to life.

2. **Scalability**: As businesses grow, their website needs may evolve. Wix Code allows for scalable development, enabling users to continuously add new features and functionalities to their websites without limitations. This ensures that the website can adapt to changing business needs over time.

3. **Time and Cost Savings**: With Wix Code, users can achieve advanced customization without the need for extensive coding knowledge or hiring a developer. This saves both time and costs associated with custom development. The intuitive development environment and drag-and-drop interface make it accessible to users with varying technical backgrounds.

4. **Improved User Experience**: Advanced customization options enable website owners to create a unique and engaging user experience. By adding interactive elements, dynamic content,

and personalized functionalities, visitors are more likely to stay on the site, explore further, and convert into customers.

Using Wix App Market for Additional Functionality

The Wix App Market is a curated collection of third-party applications and services that can be integrated seamlessly into Wix websites. It provides users with a wide range of additional functionalities and tools to enhance their websites without the need for extensive coding or development skills. With the App Market, users can easily add features such as contact forms, live chat support, e-commerce capabilities, social media integrations, and much more.

Extending Functionality with the Wix App Market

The Wix App Market offers a diverse selection of apps that can be easily installed and integrated into a Wix website. Some popular categories of apps include:

1. **Communication and Support**: These apps provide tools for engaging with website visitors and offering support. Live chat apps enable real-time communication, while contact form apps allow users to create custom forms for capturing user inquiries. Additionally, help desk and ticketing apps streamline customer support processes.

2. **E-commerce**: The App Market offers various e-commerce apps to enhance online selling capabilities. Users can find apps for inventory management, order tracking, payment gateways, product reviews, and more. These apps enable website owners to create robust online stores and optimize the shopping experience for their customers.

3. **Marketing and Social Media**: Apps in this category help users with marketing automation, email campaigns, social media integrations, and analytics. Website owners can track visitor behavior, run targeted campaigns, and optimize their marketing efforts using these tools. Social media integrations allow for seamless sharing and interaction between the website and popular social platforms.

4. **Design and Customization**: Users can find apps that offer additional design elements, templates, and customization options. These apps enable users to enhance the visual appeal of their websites, create unique layouts, and add interactive features. From image galleries to animation tools, these apps provide creative ways to customize the website's appearance.

Benefits of Using the Wix App Market

The Wix App Market brings several benefits to users looking to extend their website's functionality:

1. **Easy Integration**: Apps from the Wix App Market can be seamlessly integrated into a Wix website

with just a few clicks. The integration process is user-friendly, and no coding skills are required. Users can quickly install, configure, and start using the desired app without any technical hurdles.

2. **Time and Cost Savings**: By leveraging apps from the App Market, users can save time and costs associated with custom development. Instead of building functionalities from scratch, users can choose from a wide range of pre-built solutions. This allows them to focus on other aspects of their website while still benefiting from additional features.

3. **Scalability**: The App Market offers a variety of apps that cater to different needs and stages of a website's growth. As businesses evolve, users can easily explore and install new apps to meet changing requirements. This scalability ensures that the website remains adaptable and can scale with the business.

4. **Quality and Reliability**: Apps featured in the Wix App Market undergo a review process to ensure quality and reliability. This provides users with confidence in the performance and security of the installed apps. Additionally, the App Market offers user reviews and ratings, enabling users to make informed decisions when choosing an app.

Utilizing Wix Ascend for Marketing Automation

Wix Ascend is a powerful suite of marketing tools offered by Wix. It is designed to help website owners automate and streamline their marketing efforts, allowing them to effectively engage with their audience, drive conversions, and grow their online presence. With Wix Ascend, users can leverage a range of features such as email marketing, social media posting, live chat, and customer relationship management (CRM) to enhance their marketing strategies.

Key Features of Wix Ascend

Wix Ascend provides several key features that enable effective marketing automation:

1. **Email Marketing**: Users can create and send personalized email campaigns to engage with their subscribers and customers. Wix Ascend offers professional email templates, segmentation options, and automation tools to streamline the email marketing process. Users can track email performance, analyze results, and optimize their campaigns based on valuable insights.

2. **Social Media Posting**: Wix Ascend allows users to schedule and automate their social media posts across popular platforms such as Facebook, Instagram, and Twitter. This feature enables consistent and strategic social media presence, saving time and effort in manually posting content. Users can plan their content calendar, create engaging posts, and monitor social media interactions within the Wix dashboard.

3. **Live Chat**: Wix Ascend's live chat feature enables

real-time communication with website visitors. Users can engage with potential customers, provide instant support, and answer inquiries directly from their Wix dashboard or mobile app. The live chat functionality enhances customer service and can help increase conversion rates by addressing visitor questions or concerns promptly.

4. **CRM Tools**: Wix Ascend provides a built-in CRM system to manage customer relationships effectively. Users can organize customer data, track interactions, and create customer profiles with valuable insights. This allows for targeted marketing campaigns, personalized communication, and improved customer retention strategies.

Benefits of Wix Ascend for Marketing Automation

Utilizing Wix Ascend for marketing automation brings several benefits to website owners:

1. **Streamlined Marketing Efforts**: Wix Ascend centralizes various marketing tools into a single platform, simplifying marketing workflows. Users can manage their email campaigns, social media posts, live chat interactions, and CRM data from one place. This streamlines processes and saves time by eliminating the need to switch between multiple platforms or applications.

2. **Personalized Communication**: With Wix Ascend, users can segment their audience and send personalized messages based on specific criteria.

By tailoring content to individual interests and behaviors, website owners can deliver relevant and targeted marketing campaigns. This personalized approach enhances customer engagement and improves the chances of conversion.

3. **Improved Lead Generation**: Wix Ascend's marketing automation features help in capturing and nurturing leads effectively. By utilizing tools such as email opt-in forms, lead capture pop-ups, and automated follow-up sequences, users can generate more leads and move them through the sales funnel. The automation capabilities save time and ensure consistent lead nurturing efforts.

4. **Data-Driven Insights**: Wix Ascend provides valuable data and analytics to track marketing performance. Users can measure email open rates, click-through rates, social media engagement, and other key metrics. These insights help in understanding the effectiveness of marketing campaigns, identifying areas for improvement, and making data-driven decisions for future strategies.

Implementing Analytics and Tracking

Analytics and tracking play a crucial role in understanding website performance, user behavior, and the effectiveness of marketing efforts. Wix offers robust built-in analytics tools that enable website owners to gather data, gain insights, and make informed decisions to optimize their websites.

Wix Analytics Features

Wix Analytics provides a range of features to track and analyze website performance:

1. **Visitor Analytics**: Wix allows users to track visitor metrics such as the number of visitors, unique visitors, page views, and bounce rates. These insights provide a comprehensive overview of website traffic and engagement. Users can identify popular pages, understand visitor behavior, and make data-backed decisions to improve the user experience.

2. **Conversion Tracking**: Wix Analytics enables conversion tracking, allowing users to measure and analyze specific actions taken by visitors, such as form submissions, purchases, or newsletter sign-ups. This feature helps in understanding the effectiveness of marketing campaigns and optimizing conversion funnels.

3. **SEO Analytics**: Wix provides SEO analytics to monitor website visibility and performance in search engines. Users can track keyword rankings, organic traffic, and search impressions. This information helps in optimizing website content, improving search engine rankings, and driving organic traffic.

4. **Marketing Integration**: Wix Analytics seamlessly integrates with other marketing tools and platforms, such as Google Analytics and Facebook

Pixel. Users can connect their accounts to gather additional data and insights. These integrations provide a holistic view of website performance and enable more comprehensive analysis.

Benefits of Analytics and Tracking with Wix

Implementing analytics and tracking with Wix offers several benefits to website owners:

1. **Data-Driven Decision Making**: Wix Analytics provides valuable data and insights that empower users to make informed decisions. By analyzing visitor behavior, conversion rates, and SEO performance, users can identify strengths, weaknesses, and areas for improvement. This data-driven approach helps in optimizing the website, content, and marketing strategies.

2. **Understanding User Behavior**: Wix Analytics helps in understanding how visitors interact with the website. Users can identify popular pages, entry points, exit points, and navigation patterns. This information helps in optimizing the user experience, improving website structure, and identifying content that resonates with visitors.

3. **Optimizing Marketing Efforts**: Analytics and tracking enable users to measure the effectiveness of their marketing campaigns. Users can track conversions, identify high-performing channels, and make data-backed decisions to optimize marketing budgets. By understanding which channels and campaigns drive the most valuable results, users can focus their efforts and resources

accordingly.

4. **Continuous Improvement**: With Wix Analytics, website owners can monitor website performance over time. Regular tracking and analysis allow users to identify trends, spot changes in visitor behavior, and adapt their strategies accordingly. This iterative approach to website optimization ensures continuous improvement and better alignment with business goals.

Managing and Updating Your Website

Managing and updating a website is essential to ensure its functionality, security, and relevance over time. With Wix, website owners have access to user-friendly tools and features that make managing and updating their websites a seamless process.

Wix Website Management Features

Wix offers several features that facilitate website management and updates:

1. **Intuitive Website Editor**: Wix provides an intuitive drag-and-drop website editor that allows users to easily make changes to their website's design and content. Users can add new elements, edit existing ones, and rearrange the layout with a simple and user-friendly interface. This flexibility enables website owners to keep their websites up to date and visually appealing.

2. **Content Management System (CMS)**: Wix's built-in CMS makes it easy to manage website content. Users can create and edit pages, publish blog posts, and update product listings for e-commerce websites. The CMS provides a structured and organized approach to content management, ensuring consistency and ease of navigation for visitors.

3. **Mobile Optimization**: Wix automatically optimizes websites for mobile devices, ensuring a seamless browsing experience across different screen sizes. Website owners don't have to worry about separately managing a mobile version of their site. Wix takes care of responsive design, allowing users to focus on creating and updating content without compromising mobile user experience.

4. **App and Plugin Management**: Wix allows users to manage the apps and plugins installed on their websites. Users can easily add or remove apps from the Wix App Market, enabling them to expand functionality or remove features that are no longer needed. This flexibility ensures that the website's features and capabilities can be adapted as business needs evolve.

5. **Scheduled Publishing**: Wix allows users to schedule content updates and changes to be published at specific times. This feature is particularly useful for time-sensitive announcements, limited-time promotions, or blog posts that need to be published in advance. Website owners can set up their updates in

advance, ensuring timely publication without the need for manual intervention.

Benefits of Website Management with Wix

Managing and updating a website using Wix provides several benefits:

1. **User-Friendly Interface**: Wix's intuitive interface and drag-and-drop editor make it easy for website owners, regardless of their technical skills, to manage and update their websites. The user-friendly environment reduces the learning curve and empowers users to make changes and updates independently.

2. **Time and Cost Efficiency**: With Wix, website owners can manage and update their websites efficiently, saving both time and costs. The user-friendly interface eliminates the need for extensive coding or technical expertise. Website owners can focus on creating and updating content without the need for hiring external developers or spending hours on complex manual updates.

3. **Real-Time Updates**: Wix allows website owners to make changes in real-time. Whether it's updating product information, publishing blog posts, or adding new pages, the changes are instantly reflected on the live website. This immediate updating capability ensures that visitors see the most up-to-date information and enhances the user experience.

4. **Security and Stability**: Wix takes care of website security and stability, including regular updates and patches to protect against potential vulnerabilities. Website owners can rely on Wix's infrastructure and dedicated security measures, allowing them to focus on managing and updating their content without worrying about technical security aspects.

5. **Collaboration**: Wix enables collaboration by allowing multiple users to work on the same website simultaneously. Website owners can invite team members or external collaborators to contribute to content creation and website management. This collaborative environment enhances productivity and facilitates efficient website updates.

CHAPTER SIX

Launching and Promoting Your Website

Testing and Previewing Your Website

When it comes to creating a website, testing and previewing are crucial steps in ensuring a seamless user experience. It allows you to identify and fix any issues before launching your website to the public. Here are some key aspects to consider when testing and previewing your website.

1. **Browser Compatibility**: Test your website on different browsers such as Google Chrome, Mozilla Firefox, Safari, and Microsoft Edge. Each browser may interpret and display your website's content differently, so it's important to ensure consistency across all major browsers.

2. **Responsiveness**: With the increasing use of mobile devices, it's essential to test your website's responsiveness. Your website should adapt and

display correctly on various screen sizes, including smartphones and tablets. This ensures optimal user experience regardless of the device being used.

3. **Functionality**: Test all interactive elements on your website, such as buttons, forms, and navigation menus, to ensure they are working as intended. Check for broken links, missing images, or any other functionality issues that may hinder user experience.

4. **Load Time**: Website speed is crucial for user satisfaction and search engine optimization. Test your website's load time using tools like Google PageSpeed Insights or GTmetrix. Optimize images, minimize code, and leverage caching to improve performance.

5. **Content Review**: Proofread all the content on your website to ensure accuracy, clarity, and proper grammar. Check for any outdated information or broken paragraphs that may negatively impact your website's credibility.

6. **Usability Testing**: Conduct usability testing with a small group of individuals who represent your target audience. Observe how they navigate your website and gather feedback on its ease of use, clarity of information, and overall user experience. This feedback can be invaluable in identifying areas for improvement.

Remember, testing and previewing your website should be an iterative process. Make adjustments based on feedback and conduct additional rounds of testing to ensure a polished final product.

Connecting Your Domain

Once you have designed and developed your website, the next step is to connect it to a domain. A domain is the unique address that users will type into their browsers to access your website. Here's a step-by-step guide to connecting your domain:

1. **Choose a Domain Registrar**: Select a reputable domain registrar to purchase your domain. Popular domain registrars include GoDaddy, Namecheap, and Google Domains. Compare prices and features to make an informed choice.

2. **Domain Registration**: Follow the registrar's instructions to register your chosen domain. Provide the necessary information, including your contact details and payment information. Keep in mind that domain registration fees are typically renewed annually.

3. **DNS Configuration**: Once you have registered your domain, you need to configure the Domain Name System (DNS) settings. This involves linking your domain to the web server where your website is hosted. Consult your web hosting provider for the specific DNS settings you need to configure.

4. **Nameservers**: Update the nameservers of your

domain to point to your web hosting provider's nameservers. This ensures that when someone types your domain into their browser, it will direct them to the correct web server where your website is hosted.

5. **Propagation Time**: DNS changes may take some time to propagate across the internet. It can range from a few minutes to 48 hours. During this time, some users may still be directed to the old server while others see the new one. Be patient and allow sufficient time for the changes to take effect.

6. **Verification**: After the DNS changes have propagated, verify that your domain is connected to your website correctly. Type your domain into a browser and check if your website loads as expected. Test different pages and functionalities to ensure everything is working properly.

Connecting your domain is an important step in establishing your online presence. Take the time to follow these steps carefully to ensure a smooth transition from domain registration to website hosting.

Going Live with Your Website

Once you have thoroughly tested your website and connected your domain, it's time to go live and make your website accessible to the public. Here's a guide on how to successfully launch your website:

1. **Backup Your Website**: Before making any changes, create a backup of your website files and database. This ensures that you have a copy of your website in case anything goes wrong during the launch process.

2. **Remove Test Pages and Content**: Delete any placeholder or test content that you used during the development phase. Make sure that your website only displays finalized and relevant information.

3. **Check Permissions and Security**: Ensure that your website's permissions and security settings are correctly configured. Set appropriate file permissions to prevent unauthorized access and protect sensitive data.

4. **Submit Sitemap to Search Engines**: Generate a sitemap for your website and submit it to search engines like Google, Bing, and Yahoo. This helps search engines discover and index your website's pages, improving your online visibility.

5. **Set up Analytics**: Install a web analytics tool like Google Analytics to track and analyze your website's performance. This provides valuable insights into your website's traffic, user behavior, and conversion rates.

6. **Promote Your Website**: Spread the word about your newly launched website through various marketing channels. Implement marketing

strategies such as social media promotion, email marketing, and search engine marketing (which we will explore in the following sections) to attract visitors and increase engagement.

Remember to continuously monitor your website after it goes live. Regularly update your content, fix any issues that arise, and stay informed about the latest web development best practices to ensure a successful online presence.

Implementing Marketing Strategies

Marketing plays a crucial role in driving traffic and increasing the visibility of your website. Here are some effective marketing strategies to implement:

1. **Identify Your Target Audience**: Clearly define your target audience based on demographics, interests, and behavior. This allows you to tailor your marketing efforts to reach the right people.

2. **Develop a Marketing Plan**: Create a comprehensive marketing plan that outlines your goals, target audience, messaging, and promotional channels. Set specific objectives and allocate resources accordingly.

3. **Content Marketing**: Develop high-quality content that provides value to your audience. Create blog posts, articles, videos, or infographics that address their pain points, answer their questions, and establish you as an authority in your industry.

4. **Search Engine Optimization (SEO)**: Optimize your website for search engines to improve organic visibility. Conduct keyword research, optimize meta tags, create quality backlinks, and ensure your website follows SEO best practices.

5. **Paid Advertising**: Consider using paid advertising platforms such as Google Ads or social media advertising to reach a wider audience. Set a budget, define target demographics, and create compelling ad campaigns that drive traffic to your website.

6. **Measure and Analyze**: Regularly monitor and analyze the effectiveness of your marketing strategies. Track key metrics such as website traffic, conversion rates, engagement, and ROI. Use this data to refine your marketing efforts and improve results over time.

By implementing a well-rounded marketing strategy, you can effectively promote your website, attract your target audience, and achieve your business objectives.

Social Media Promotion

Social media platforms provide excellent opportunities for promoting your website and engaging with your audience. Here's how you can effectively promote your website through social media:

1. **Choose the Right Platforms**: Identify the social media platforms that align with your target

audience and business goals. Popular options include Facebook, Instagram, Twitter, LinkedIn, and Pinterest. Each platform caters to different demographics and content types, so choose wisely.

2. **Create Engaging Content**: Develop content that resonates with your audience and encourages interaction. Share blog posts, articles, images, videos, and infographics that provide value, entertain, or inform. Use compelling visuals and engaging captions to capture attention.

3. **Build a Community**: Foster a sense of community by actively engaging with your followers. Respond to comments, messages, and mentions. Encourage discussions, ask questions, and encourage user-generated content. Building relationships with your audience helps establish brand loyalty.

4. **Hashtags and Keywords**: Utilize relevant hashtags and keywords to increase the visibility of your social media posts. Research popular hashtags in your industry and incorporate them strategically. This helps users discover your content and join relevant conversations.

5. **Collaborate with Influencers**: Partner with influencers in your industry who have a significant following and credibility. Collaborating with influencers allows you to tap into their audience and gain exposure for your website. Seek influencers whose values align with your brand.

6. **Paid Advertising**: Consider running targeted social media ad campaigns to reach a wider audience. Social media platforms offer advanced targeting options based on demographics, interests, and behaviors. Set specific goals, allocate a budget, and monitor campaign performance.

7. **Analytics and Optimization**: Use social media analytics tools to track the performance of your posts and campaigns. Monitor engagement metrics, follower growth, and click-through rates. Analyze the data to understand what content resonates best with your audience and optimize your social media strategy accordingly.

Remember to maintain consistency in your social media presence. Regularly update your profiles, share valuable content, and engage with your audience. Social media promotion is an ongoing process that requires active management and adaptation to stay relevant.

Email Marketing

Email marketing remains one of the most effective ways to reach and engage your audience. Here's how to leverage email marketing to promote your website:

1. **Build an Email List**: Start by building an opt-in email list of subscribers who are interested in your content or products. Offer incentives such as exclusive content, discounts, or freebies

to encourage sign-ups. Ensure compliance with email marketing regulations like GDPR and CAN-SPAM.

2. **Segmentation**: Segment your email list based on demographics, interests, or behaviors. This allows you to send targeted and personalized content that resonates with each segment. Tailored emails have higher open rates and click-through rates.

3. **Compelling Subject Lines**: Craft attention-grabbing subject lines that entice recipients to open your emails. Keep them concise, intriguing, and relevant to the content inside. Experiment with different subject line strategies and analyze open rates to optimize performance.

4. **Valuable Content**: Provide valuable and relevant content in your emails. This can include blog posts, product updates, industry news, tutorials, or exclusive offers. The content should be tailored to your subscribers' interests and address their pain points.

5. **Call-to-Action (CTA)**: Include clear and compelling CTAs in your emails to direct subscribers to your website. Whether it's to read a blog post, make a purchase, or sign up for an event, a strong CTA encourages action. Use contrasting colors, persuasive copy, and a prominent placement to make your CTAs stand out.

6. **Automation and Personalization**: Utilize email marketing automation tools to streamline your campaigns and deliver personalized

experiences. Set up automated welcome emails, abandoned cart reminders, or birthday greetings. Personalization helps build relationships and increase conversions.

7. **A/B Testing**: Experiment with different email elements, such as subject lines, CTAs, layouts, or visuals, through A/B testing. Split your email list and test two variations to determine which performs better. Use the insights to refine your email marketing strategy.

8. **Analytics and Optimization**: Track key metrics like open rates, click-through rates, conversion rates, and unsubscribe rates. Analyze the data to understand what resonates with your audience and optimize your email campaigns accordingly. Regularly clean your email list to remove inactive subscribers.

Email marketing is a powerful tool for nurturing relationships, driving traffic, and boosting conversions. With thoughtful planning, quality content, and strategic optimization, you can effectively promote your website through email campaigns.

Search Engine Marketing

Search Engine Marketing (SEM) involves promoting your website through paid advertising on search engines. It helps increase visibility, drive targeted traffic, and generate leads. Here are the key steps to implement an SEM strategy:

1. **Keyword Research**: Identify relevant keywords that align with your business, products, or services. Use keyword research tools like Google Keyword Planner or SEMrush to discover high-volume and low-competition keywords. Target a mix of short-tail and long-tail keywords to capture different user search intents.

2. **Ad Campaign Creation**: Set up your ad campaigns on search engine advertising platforms like Google Ads or Microsoft Advertising. Create compelling ad copy that highlights your unique selling points and encourages users to click. Select appropriate targeting options such as location, demographics, and interests.

3. **Budget Allocation**: Determine your advertising budget based on your goals and the competitiveness of your industry. Allocate your budget strategically across different campaigns and keywords. Monitor your spending and adjust bids to optimize your return on investment (ROI).

4. **Landing Page Optimization**: Design and optimize landing pages that align with your ad campaigns. Ensure your landing pages have clear messaging, strong CTAs, and relevant content. Use A/B testing to experiment with different elements and improve conversion rates.

5. **Conversion Tracking**: Implement conversion tracking on your website to measure the success

of your SEM campaigns. Set up tracking pixels or codes to track actions such as form submissions, purchases, or newsletter sign-ups. Analyze the data to evaluate campaign performance and make data-driven decisions.

6. **Ad Performance Monitoring**: Monitor the performance of your ads regularly. Track metrics like click-through rates (CTR), conversion rates, cost per acquisition (CPA), and return on ad spend (ROAS). Identify underperforming ads or keywords and make adjustments to improve results.

7. **Remarketing**: Implement remarketing campaigns to target users who have previously visited your website. Show them relevant ads to re-engage and encourage them to return. Remarketing can be a powerful tool for increasing conversions and improving overall campaign performance.

SEM can provide immediate visibility and targeted traffic to your website. However, it requires ongoing monitoring, optimization, and budget management to ensure a successful campaign.

CHAPTER SEVEN

Troubleshooting and Support

Common Issues and Solutions

In today's fast-paced digital world, website owners often encounter common issues that can hinder their online presence. However, with the right knowledge and resources, many of these challenges can be resolved effectively. This article aims to explore some of the common issues faced by website owners and provide practical solutions to address them.

Slow Website Performance

Slow website performance is a frequent complaint among website owners. It can lead to frustrated visitors who may leave the site before it fully loads, negatively impacting user experience and conversion rates. There are several reasons why a website may be slow, including:

1. **Large Image Sizes**: Images that are not optimized for web can significantly slow down a website. To resolve this issue, website owners should compress their images without sacrificing quality or consider using image optimization tools.

2. **Caching and Content Delivery**: Implementing caching mechanisms and utilizing Content Delivery Networks (CDNs) can improve website speed by serving cached content from servers located closer to the user.

3. **Excessive Plugins and Scripts**: Having an excessive number of plugins and scripts can weigh down a website. Website owners should regularly review and remove unnecessary plugins and scripts to improve website performance.

4. **Server Configuration**: Inadequate server resources or improper server configuration can impact website speed. It is essential to ensure that the hosting provider offers sufficient resources and optimize the server configuration for better performance.

Mobile Responsiveness

As the number of mobile users continues to rise, having a **mobile-responsive website** is crucial for providing an optimal user experience. Failure to address this issue can result in high bounce rates and a loss of potential customers. Here are some solutions to improve mobile responsiveness:

1. **Responsive Design**: Implementing a responsive design ensures that the website adapts to different screen sizes and devices. This approach eliminates the need for maintaining separate mobile and desktop versions of the website.

2. **Testing on Multiple Devices**: It's important to test the website on various devices and screen sizes to identify any responsiveness issues. This can be done manually or by utilizing testing tools that simulate different devices.

3. **Optimized Media Queries**: Media queries allow websites to apply different styles based on screen size. Optimizing media queries ensures that content is displayed correctly and efficiently on different devices.

4. **User-friendly Navigation**: Simplify the navigation menu on mobile devices to make it easy for users to find information quickly. Utilize collapsible menus or hamburger icons to save screen space.

SEO Optimization

Search Engine Optimization (SEO) plays a crucial role in driving organic traffic to a website. However, many website owners struggle with optimizing their sites for search engines. Here are some solutions to common SEO issues:

1. **Keyword Research**: Conduct thorough keyword research to identify relevant keywords and

phrases that potential visitors might use to find your website. Utilize keyword research tools to determine search volumes and competition levels.

2. **Quality Content**: Create high-quality, informative, and engaging content that aligns with your target audience's interests. Incorporate relevant keywords naturally within the content while avoiding keyword stuffing.

3. **Meta Tags and Descriptions**: Optimize meta tags and descriptions to accurately describe the content of each page. Include relevant keywords while ensuring the descriptions are compelling and encourage click-throughs from search engine results.

4. **Page Load Speed**: As mentioned earlier, website speed is crucial for SEO. Optimize images, enable caching, and minify CSS and JavaScript files to improve page load speed, which positively impacts search engine rankings.

Wix Support Resources

Wix provides a range of **support resources** to help users navigate and overcome challenges while using their platform. These resources are designed to assist users in resolving common issues and provide guidance for achieving their website goals. Some of the key support resources offered by Wix include:

1. **Help Center**: Wix's Help Center is a comprehensive knowledge base that covers various topics related to website creation, design, and management. It provides step-by-step tutorials, troubleshooting guides, and answers to frequently asked questions.

2. **Video Tutorials**: Wix offers a collection of video tutorials that visually guide users through different aspects of building and maintaining a website. These tutorials cover topics such as website design, customization, and SEO optimization.

3. **Wix Blog**: The Wix Blog is a valuable resource that offers tips, insights, and best practices for website owners. It covers a wide range of topics, including marketing strategies, design trends, and industry-specific advice.

4. **Support Tickets and Live Chat**: For personalized assistance, users can submit support tickets or engage in live chat sessions with Wix's customer support team. These channels allow users to get direct help for specific issues they may encounter.

Community Forums and Help Center

In addition to official support resources, Wix also fosters a vibrant **community forums** and **Help Center** where users can seek advice, share experiences, and learn from fellow website owners. These platforms offer several benefits:

1. **Peer-to-Peer Support**: Community forums enable users to interact with other Wix users who may have faced similar challenges. It provides an opportunity to seek advice, share solutions, and learn from the experiences of others.

2. **Knowledge Sharing**: Users can share their insights, tips, and best practices with the community, fostering a collaborative environment where everyone can benefit from collective knowledge.

3. **Troubleshooting Guides**: The Help Center within the community forums often contains troubleshooting guides contributed by experienced users. These guides offer step-by-step instructions and workarounds for specific issues.

4. **Wix Experts**: The community forums also showcase Wix Experts, professionals who are well-versed in the platform. Users can reach out to these experts for personalized assistance and guidance.

In conclusion, website owners often encounter common issues that can affect their online presence. However, with the right solutions, these challenges can be overcome. By addressing slow website performance, optimizing mobile responsiveness, implementing effective SEO strategies, and utilizing Wix's support resources and community forums, website owners can enhance their websites and provide a better user experience for their visitors.

CONCLUSION

Recap of Key Points

In any form of communication, whether it's a presentation, article, or conversation, it's crucial to ensure that key points are effectively conveyed and understood by the audience. A recap of key points serves as a powerful tool to reinforce the main ideas and takeaways. By summarizing and highlighting the most important information, a recap can enhance comprehension and leave a lasting impact on the listeners or readers.

When delivering a recap of key points, there are several strategies you can employ to make it engaging and memorable. Let's explore some of these techniques:

1. **Clear and Concise Summary**: Begin the recap by providing a clear and concise summary of the main points discussed. Avoid going into excessive detail at this stage, as the purpose is to provide

a brief overview that refreshes the audience's memory.

2. **Visual Aids**: Incorporating visual aids such as charts, graphs, or diagrams can enhance the recap by presenting information in a visually appealing manner. Visuals can aid in retention and help the audience visualize the key points more effectively.

3. **Highlighting the Highlights**: Identify the most significant points from the previous discussion or presentation and emphasize them during the recap. By focusing on these highlights, you draw attention to the core concepts and ensure they resonate with the audience.

4. **Repetition with Variation**: Repeat the key points multiple times throughout the recap, but introduce slight variations in your phrasing or examples. This technique helps reinforce the ideas while keeping the recap interesting and engaging.

5. **Use of Analogies or Stories**: Incorporate analogies or storytelling techniques to illustrate the key points. Analogies make complex concepts more relatable, while stories create a narrative that captivates the audience's attention and makes the recap more memorable.

6. **Interactive Recap**: Encourage audience participation by involving them in the recap process. Ask questions related to the key points and allow them to share their understanding or insights. This interactive approach creates a sense of engagement and deepens their connection

with the material.

7. **Visual or Verbal Cues**: Utilize visual or verbal cues to signal transitions between key points during the recap. This helps the audience follow along and keeps them oriented within the larger context of the discussion.

A well-executed recap of key points ensures that the audience leaves with a solid understanding of the main ideas and takeaways. By employing various techniques to make the recap engaging and memorable, you can increase the likelihood of retaining the information and inspiring action based on the communicated message.

Encouragement to Take Action

When crafting any form of persuasive communication, it's essential to not only inform but also inspire action in your audience. Encouraging individuals to take action is a powerful way to motivate them to make a change, adopt a new behavior, or pursue a specific goal. Here are some effective strategies for encouraging action:

1. **Clear and Compelling Call-to-Action**: A call-to-action (CTA) is a direct request for the audience to take a specific step. Make your CTA clear, concise, and compelling. Clearly communicate what you want your audience to do and why it's beneficial for them.

2. **Highlight the Benefits**: Clearly articulate the benefits or advantages that the audience will gain by taking the desired action. Paint a vivid picture of the positive outcomes and emphasize how their lives will improve as a result. People are more likely to take action when they see the personal value in doing so.

3. **Create a Sense of Urgency**: Instill a sense of urgency by conveying the importance of taking action promptly. Highlight any time-sensitive factors or potential consequences of inaction. When people feel that there is a limited window of opportunity, they are more likely to act swiftly.

4. **Provide Social Proof**: Humans are influenced by the actions and behaviors of others. Share testimonials, success stories, or statistics that demonstrate how others have benefited from taking similar actions. Social proof helps build trust and confidence, making it easier for individuals to take the leap themselves.

5. **Break Down Barriers**: Identify and address potential barriers or objections that may prevent people from taking action. Offer solutions, resources, or guidance to help individuals overcome these obstacles. By providing support and removing roadblocks, you increase the likelihood of action.

6. **Invoke Emotion**: Appeal to the emotions of your audience by evoking feelings of excitement, inspiration, or even a sense of responsibility. Emotional connections can be powerful catalysts for action, as they create a personal investment

and drive individuals to make a difference.

7. **Follow-up and Support**: Offer ongoing support and follow-up to individuals who take action. This can include additional resources, guidance, or even a community where they can connect with like-minded individuals. By providing ongoing support, you foster a sense of accountability and increase the chances of sustained action.

Remember, effective encouragement to take action goes beyond simply providing information. It requires engaging the audience on an emotional level, addressing their concerns, and clearly communicating the benefits of action. By implementing these strategies, you can inspire your audience to move from passive recipients of information to active participants in creating change.

www.ingramcontent.com/pod-product-compliance
Lightning Source LLC
LaVergne TN
LVHW051746050326
832903LV00029B/2760